You Wrote It, Now What?

ELSA KURT

ELSA KURT

Copyright © by Bill 2018 Elsa Kurt
All rights reserved. No part of this publication may be reproduced, distributed, or transmitted in any form or by any means, including photocopying, recording, or other electronic or mechanical methods, without the prior written permission of the publisher, except in the case of brief quotations embodied in critical reviews and certain other noncommercial uses permitted by copyright law. For permission requests, write to the publisher, addressed "Attention: Permissions Coordinator," at the address below.

authorelsakurt@gmail.com

Ordering Information:
Quantity sales. Special discounts are available on quantity purchases by corporations, associations, and others. For details, contact the publisher at the address above.
Orders by U.S. trade bookstores and wholesalers. Please contact authorelsakurt@gmail.com or visit www.elsakurt.com.

Printed in the United States of America

ISBN: 9781790353873

ELSA KURT

CONTENTS

CONTENTS v

DEDICATION vii

ACKNOWLEDGMENTS ix

1 MY 'WHY' 1

2 ON WRITING 6

3 ON WRITING, PART TWO 14

4 CONJUNCTION FUNCTION 20

5 BETA, BABY 24

6 INDIE OR TRADITIONAL 29

7 ANCHORS AWEIGH 32

8 NAVIGATING THE CIRCUIT 39

9 NAVIGATING THE CIRCUIT, PART TWO 47

10 OVERALL PRESENTATION 53

11 YOU'RE READY 56

12 FINAL NOTES 61

ABOUT THE AUTHOR 71

ELSA KURT

DEDICATION

To aspiring writers. There's no better time than now to accomplish your writing goals.

ELSA KURT

ACKNOWLEDGMENTS

I have been so incredibly fortunate in life and on this writing and publishing journey. There are countless people to thank, from family and friends to the amazing author community I get to be a part of. Through my presentations of You Wrote It, Now What, and now with this book, I get the chance to pay forward some of my good fortunes to you, the aspiring or new writer. Thank you to all who've inspired and encouraged me and thank you to those who doubted me. You're all instrumental in my desire and determination to succeed and give back.

ELSA KURT

"Quiet people have the loudest minds."

Stephen King

1 MY 'WHY'

When I began writing with intent—intent to publish, to share—I had no ever-loving idea what I was doing. I figuratively jumped face first and flew by the seat of my pants through the whole process. I made a bunch of mistakes, did things ass-backward, and learned as I went along.

Essentially, I put myself through a crash course in all things writing, publishing, and self-promoting.

I'm still learning, growing, and improving, as we all should. Through sharing my experiences, I've found great satisfaction in helping other aspiring authors begin their journey. In writing this book, I hope to send many more on their path to writing with intent. The following pages will walk you through each phase of the process. We'll tackle the most common obstacles and roadblocks faced by nearly every writer. Whether it be insecurity and self-doubt, or mere lack of know-how, we'll address and conquer each concern.

No matter if you've written your first book or just have an idea for one, there is no better time than right now to take your next steps. In my presentations, I like to take my writers on what I call, 'the scenic route' of the writing, publishing, and self-promoting journey.

I shamelessly share my embarrassing mistakes and hard-learned lessons, all in hopes of making *their* writing journey go more smoothly than mine did. What I always say at the beginning of each session is this: *I am not an expert on anything other than my own experiences.* As I mentioned, I jumped face first into publishing my first book, and then I flew by the seat of my pants, figuring it all out as I went. Would I recommend my early method? Definitely not. Which is reason number one of why I want to help you.

The second, equally important reason stems from the many book signing events I've done over the years. At each, there is always, *always* someone who approaches me with a glint in their eye and a nervous hesitation. While I'd love to say that it's because they're overcome with excitement at meeting Author Elsa Kurt... it's not that. Inevitably they tell me one of two things:

One: "You know, I've written a book, but I really don't know what to do with it (or they're afraid to put it out there)"

Two: "I've had this idea for a book forever, but..." (insert various reasons that all really boil down to fear.)

This floors and excites me every time. *I was once them. I understand.* I spent *years* holding myself back from my dream. Then, one day, I gave myself permission to dare, to *do*. I stopped letting self-doubt and insecurity be the damn boss of me. I was forty-one, and I was going to write with intent.

I'd be completely remiss to not mention that I was blessed then and now to have the unwavering support and encouragement of my husband, which is still invaluable to my pursuits. Perhaps it is because of my good fortune and my overwhelming gratitude that I want to essentially pay it forward to you. While I may not (I definitely do not) have all the answers for you, I have the means to get you well on your way. The rest, as they say, is up to you.

In the following pages, I'll be reiterating and expanding on those earlier mentioned presentation points. We'll dive into the writing routine, then to sparking your creativity, and on to publishing options. After that, self-promotion/marketing, and navigations the fair/festival/ convention circuits and event etiquette (yes, it's a thing). By the end of this book, I believe you'll be motivated to be truly on your way to pursuing your writing ambitions.

Writing a novel is like driving a car at night. You can only see as far as your headlights, but you can make the whole trip that way.
– E. L. Doctorow

2 ON WRITING

Our first step in the process revolves around setting a writing routine. Allow me a quick, relevant story about when I began writing my first novel. I had this notion that I could only write when the 'creative mood hit me,' and that creativity wasn't something that could be scheduled or planned. Well, surprise, surprise, I was wrong.

YOU WROTE IT, NOW WHAT?

The truth is—and if you won't take it from me, then read up on what some of the most successful authors (ahem, Stephen King, thank you) say on the subject—you need a routine. It is crucial to productivity.

I happen to be incredibly fortunate to have a block of time practically every day that I get to devote to writing. I treat it like it's my bill-paying job (one where I get to wear footy pajamas and slippers, mind you). I get my coffee, set my mood music (more on that in a moment) and sit down at my desk. Nine a.m. until 1 (or 2) p.m. I take breaks of course, but that's the habitude.

If you don't have a routine—a time, place, atmosphere—it is time to create one. What is your most conducive work environment? Are you a coffee shop guy or a library girl? Do you need absolute silence, or thrive on sights and sounds? As I mentioned above, I listen to softly playing music that evokes the mood/genre I'm writing in.

For example, when writing Mae's Café, the

central character had a passion for nineteen-forties music and styles. Since I knew I'd be spending a lot of time in her head, I played jazz and swing music from that era.

Regardless of your stylistic preferences, a routine will 'train your brain' to work on command. It's something I believed impossible, but I can attest to its amazing results. Case in point, four of my books were written in under three months, with the last taking exactly eight weeks to the day. Was is slightly grueling at times? Yes. However, I'd set a deadline for myself and was determined to stick to it.

For me, routine, goal setting, and deadlines are about as close to structure as I like. With regards to the actual writing process, you're often either one of two types: A Planner or A Pantser. Planners do just that—they plan and outline their book. The compile their research, collect their facts, organize the chapters... yawn, blah, blech. And now you've guessed which one I am. Yep, pantser all the way.

YOU WROTE IT, NOW WHAT?

The good news is, there's no right or wrong. Do what works for you. In fact, if you think a writing routine won't work for you, by all means, do it your way. But—there's always a *but*—at least give it a solid try.

Your Story

Everybody has a story to tell. Even the most ordinary of experiences can be made to seem extraordinary. It just has to be told *well*. One can relay that, *'Jack walked into the store and bought milk,'* or that, *'The icy air of the store hit Jack's sweat-streaked face. The clerk eyed him as he staggered down the aisle and mopped his brow with the hem of his shirt. The neat row of snow-white milk beckoned him. But which one should he pick?'*

Sure, our first question might be why the hell does Jack want milk on a hot day? But the second example certainly seems more intriguing than the first, doesn't it?

No matter what you write about, it needs to be engaging, relatable, moving, and compelling. So, how do you tell your story—be it fiction or factual—in a way that makes a reader want to know more? The answer, in nearly every case, is: Show, Don't Tell. As a writer, it is your task to *show* your readers the story, make them feel, see and hear everything *you* feel, see, and hear as you committed the words to the page. Imagine, if you will, that you are painting a picture, rather than telling a story.

Words and phrases like, "I thought..." or "she saw..." will turn your reader into a passive observer of the story. I won't say that verbs are your enemy...but they kinda are. Whenever possible, leave them out. (Consider using a program like Master Writer to develop new ways to describe.) For example, take these two sentences from my book A Season to Remember.

In the first draft of the story, I wrote,

Rosie **looked** in the rearview mirror. She **saw**

that her nose was red. She **said to herself**, "Not too bad, Rosie."

In the revised draft, I showed, rather than told:

"Rosabelle checked her lipstick in the little sunshine-yellow Mini Cooper's rearview mirror. She caught sight of her red-tipped nose then met her eyes in the frost-rimmed glass. "Not too bad, Rosie," she said under her breath.

These small changes have the reader—in their mind's eye—seeing the little bright car, looking up into the rearview mirror, and understanding that it's cold outside. So, instead of words being merely read, they've now had a picture painted.

There are numerous books & online resources available that give alternatives to the most commonly used gestures and actions. I highly recommend having them in your writer's toolbox. Also, taking note of sights, smells, and sounds in your own environment is helpful in expanding your creative writing.

Try not to rely on idioms or cliches. *'As big as a whale,'* or *'As blue as the sky,'* for example, are tired and lazy writing. Come up with new, vivid descriptions whenever possible.

The same notion applies to descriptive writing. I've caught myself overusing, 'washed-denim blue eyes,' and had to spend some time trying to convey the color in new, creative ways. A similar problem cropped up when I realized my characters 'sighed' way too often.

Sometimes, you'll find that a word repeats in a paragraph. For example, in Still Here, I belatedly found that I'd used the word 'water' four times in one paragraph. *Four times*. This is very irritating to the reader, even if they don't consciously realize it.

Checking for these common writing pitfalls can be tedious work, but the benefit far outweighs the trouble. It may take several passes through the manuscript to find them but making use of your navigation search tab decreases quite a bit of the time.

Highlights

Set a routine for your writing. This means, find a location, time of day, and atmosphere that makes for conducive writing

Eliminate distractions. If Facebook or text messages keep pulling your focus away, set your phone in another room, or even turn off your internet connection.

Hone your writing skills. Practice showing your story rather than telling it.

Find and edit overused words/phrases. Redundancy gets noticed. Remember to flex your brain and create new ways of saying what you want to convey.

"Half my life is an act of revision."
– John Irving

3 ON WRITING, PART TWO

So now that we've tackled and conquered the writing routine, we're ready to move on to the technical stuff. If you plan to submit your manuscript to a publishing house, please, *please* do your homework. Make sure they are reputable and established. They do not have to be one of the 'Big Five' to be legit, they just have to not ask you to pay them to print your books.

In my travels around the author event circuit, I've met some authors who've described their relationship with their 'publishers' as such: "Well, they don't actually do any promoting or editing for me. I have to do that. And once I make back the money I paid my publisher to print my books, then I'll start seeing some profit."

My friends, that's not a publisher, that's a printer. Another name you'll hear for this is 'Vanity Publisher,' or 'Vanity Press,' which are all basically the same thing: You do all the work—writing, editing, marketing—and you pay them to print your books. There are many companies out there ready and willing to take you for an expensive ride under the guise of 'helping you get your work out to the public... for an upfront fee.' I almost fell for it, too.

A few years back, I'd sent out a manuscript to a 'publishing house.' About a month later, I receive a lovely, official-looking envelope holding a very lovely looking folder with an extremely lovely looking contract inside it. After I jumped up and down for a few (several) minutes, I began to read the contract a little more critically. That was when I picked out some wording that confounded me. Specifically, it stated, that they were offering me a "*contributory* contract, as I was a new author, and they can't take the risk..."

I thought, "What the hell is a contributory contract?" Well, it basically means I'd have to pay them up front to print my books, do pretty much all my own advertising and promoting (they'd do 'some') and once I'd recouped the money spent, they'd kick in. If I recall, the amount was somewhere in the range of two to three thousand dollars.

In a nutshell, they wanted me to pay them to do exactly what I could do on my own *for free* through (then) Createspace, which is now KDP. Know this: No real publisher is going to ask you for money. Do your research, read the fine print. Don't get taken for a ride.

YOU WROTE IT, NOW WHAT?

There are some exceptions or variations of this practice. Sometimes they are actual vanity publishing houses who *do* traditionally publish authors and offer contributory contracts to those they consider 'a risk.' If you prove yourself marketable and profitable, they'll offer you a standard contract. Based on what I've read, their contracts are questionable, to say the least.

If your goal is to be traditionally published, then make sure your manuscript is up to industry (or individual publisher) standards. Typically, they accept Times New Roman, 12pt, single-spaced, but there are exceptions and variations. Today, there are numerous publishing houses that will accept unagented manuscripts, however, the Big Five (at the time of this publication) do not. Subscribing to sites like Authors Publish Magazine will put all types of opportunities in your lap.

If you have decided that independent publishing is the avenue for you, then you have *some* liberties you can take. However, choosing 'pretty' or unique fonts is highly discouraged, they are visually tiresome to the average reader's eye. As you can see, I'm fond of Calibri Light, but up until recently, I've used Times New Roman. A 12pt font is consistent. I also like a 1.15 or 1.5 spacing.

Most typically, book dimensions of either 5 x 8 or 6 x 9 are used for printing. If my book is shorter in length (200 pages or less) I like to use 5 x 8, and anything higher, I use 6 x 9.

Now, pardon my language, but I have always found formatting to be an absolute bitch. It's one of my final frontiers in educating myself in the publishing process. If you are in the same boat, I recommend using formatted templates (or getting professional help). Somehow, I still manage to run into trouble, but usually (after much swearing and threats to throw the damn computer out the window) I figure it out.

If grammar and punctuation are not your strong points, it is imperative you get help. A poorly written book with spelling, grammar, and/or excessive punctuation mistakes is the kiss of death for a book. Programs like Grammarly and Hemingway are helpful (plus your built-in spellcheck feature) in finding common mistakes. Also, taking a refresher course or reading a book on grammar can be beneficial, as well.

HIGHLIGHTS

Be Informed. Do your homework on your publishing option. There are more than you think!

Follow the guidelines. You get some allowances when independently publishing, but it's in your best interest to stay within the standard specs.

Utilize writer's resources. There are tons of books, programs, and services available to help you hone your craft. Use them!

"People on the outside think there's something magical about writing, that you go up in the attic at midnight and cast the bones and come down in the morning with a story, but it isn't like that. You sit in back of the typewriter and you work, and that's all there is to it."
— Harlan Ellison

4 CONJUNCTION FUNCTION

You've committed to writing *with intent*. Intent to publish, intent to share, intent to take your writing seriously. Congratulations, you are a writer. In the early days of my writing career, I was shy about telling anyone that. If I mentioned it at all, it would be last in line. "I'm a mom, a wife, a nanny, oh, and I wrote a book." I suppose it was because I thought they'd laugh or scoff, or worse—ask me questions about my writing.

Compounding the self-consciousness and insecurity, was my natural introverted-ness. Introversion is extremely common in our world. Books, quiet, introspection are usually our happy place, whereas large groups, excessive talking, and being the center of attention are our version of hell. Unfortunately, if you are interested in success, there is only one solution. Get over it. That may seem a bit harsh, but it's imperative that you set aside those feelings and plow through.

One thing that has helped me tremendously is having a pen name. This allows—odd as it may seem—for an alternate 'personality' to step forward. Elsa Kurt loves chatting with strangers, talking about herself and her work. Melly—the 'real' me—well, she just wants to go home and dig in her garden and be quiet. For me, having two separate sides to my personality is freeing. Will it work for you? I haven't the faintest idea. However, if you are an introvert or shy and struggling with the idea of 'putting yourself out there,' then it's worth considering.

Either way, it's time to create your social media presence. Ideally, you'll be doing this in conjunction with writing. You'll want to start building interest in both you and your book *before* you launch. The following steps are a general guideline.

- **Determine whether you are publishing under your name or a pen name.**
- **Create a website and social media accounts for your author name, use the same one across all social media.** *For example, I am @authorelsakurt across every account. I use Facebook (primarily) Instagram, Twitter, Pinterest, Amazon Author Central, Goodreads, AllAuthor, and several others—all using the same name and profile picture for instant recognition.
- **Invite friends & family to LIKE, FOLLOW, and SHARE your page**
- **Begin posting content.** This can be a combination of blurbs, teasers, general info, graphics, engaging posts. Do not inundate, though!
- **Join Facebook groups related to your topic.** But don't sales pitch them. Engage, don't pester.
- **Join your local author's association/group.** For Connecticut, it is the Connecticut Authors and Publishers Association (CAPA). This is a great way

to network and begins building your 'author tribe.'

When you are about three quarters through writing your book (of course it can be sooner and even later) you'll want to start having a cover idea in mind (and a title if you don't have one already). I recommend working with a cover artist but if you are knowledgeable in cover design, by all means, do your own. You can spend a lot, or a little depending on many factors. Personally, I've never spent more than forty-five dollars on a cover design, and many costs much less. A simple internet or social media search will supply you with plenty of designers to choose from. I use Fantasia Frog Designs for nearly all my covers and have been consistently pleased.

Don't try to figure out what other people want to hear from you; figure out what you have to say. It's the one and only thing you have to offer.
— Barbara Kingsolver

5 BETA, BABY

One of the biggest mistakes an indie pub writer can make is not having someone else read your work prior to publication. Whether you hire an editor—which can be expensive—or have 'Beta Readers' review and critique your manuscript, you absolutely must have fresh eyes on it before you publish.

It doesn't matter if you've read it one, one hundred, or one thousand times. You *will* miss typos, grammatical issues, and/or timeline discrepancies. You might have said the character has blue eyes in chapter one, but green eyes in chapter five… and so on. I know you believe you've been thorough, but it's nearly impossible. You're simply too close to the work to see it clearly. In fact, even with every failsafe, you may still go to print with an 'oops' somewhere in there. I have, and it sucks.

Fortunately, there are several methods to help lessen the likelihood. I have a process that I've only just recently instituted with my manuscripts that you may find beneficial.

- **Step One**: Step away from the manuscript. Once you've finished the first draft of your book, walk away from it for at least two to three days.

- **Step Two**: First round edits. Here is where I begin looking for 'telling' text—text that tells the story rather than shows it. I look for repetitive words and phrasing and begin the painful process of 'killing my darlings.' This merely means eliminating excess use of 'go to' words/phrases. For example, I have two words—*so* and *just*—that pop up with irritating regularity. Also, as I mentioned earlier, I have an overzealous affection for my characters sighing. This is sheer laziness and the reader will notice. Using your navigation bar to search your document for overused words is an easy trick to solve this problem. Simply 'find' and 'replace.'

- **Step Three** In this phase I like to use a program called Grammarly. It looks for spelling, punctuation, sentence structure, and more.

- **Step Four** Once you have done all this, you'll move on to Read Aloud. I use Microsoft Word, which has a read-aloud feature. With as little distraction as possible, I sit and listen to the story. Often times I hear typos that I'd missed in the previous edits (*the* that should have been *then*, etc.). Here, you'll be listening for flow and clarity, among other things. It's not unusual to realize dialogue you thought was so good in print sounds lame aloud, or that your sentence is too wordy, or too choppy for the scene. Whether you have it read aloud to you, or you read it out loud yourself, this step is crucial, so don't skip it.

- **Step Five** You've done as much editing and revising as you humanly can. Now it's time for fresh, unbiased eyes. If you've hired an editor, now it the time to submit. If you are using Beta Readers, which are secondary, non-professional, objective readers, you can send them a PDF watermarked with 'ARC' (advance readers copy). You can find them online (social media is one way to find beta readers) or ask friends or acquaintances. If you do use friends, family, or acquaintances, be sure to use ones you believe can be objective, who are well-read, and able to critique appropriately. Give them a deadline for when you'd like them back. Three weeks is reasonable.

- **Step Six** This is your final edit before submitting for publishing. You'll compile your beta edits (or editors' edits) and revise as needed. Then you'll save a .doc version and a PDF of your manuscript.

Voila! You're ready to publish. Exciting, right? I'm sure you've met some frustrations along the way, but hopefully, you've weathered them and are starting to see the light at the end of the tunnel. You're almost there. Give yourself a break. Trust that your beta readers (or editor) did their job. A bit of advice from one of my favorite authors, Neil Gaiman, with regards to criticism/critiquing:

"Remember: when people tell you something's wrong or doesn't work for them, they are almost always right. When they tell you exactly what they think is wrong and how to fix it, they are almost always wrong."

Writing is its own reward.
— Henry Miller

6 INDIE OR TRADITIONAL

Once your manuscript has passed through all the edits and proofreads, it's time to publish. One of the most common questions asked by any writer is, "How will I know for sure it's ready?" It's also one of the hardest to answer. First, decide what's holding you back from publishing. Is it fear? Doubt? Have you received mixed reviews from early (or beta) readers? Think about how *you* feel about your book. Did you put your whole attention to it and follow the steps to ensure that it is technically ready for publication? Lastly, do you believe in your work? If you can answer yes to those questions, you're as ready as you'll ever be. Sometimes, you just have to jump.

There are numerous indie publishing platforms at your disposal. Only you can decide which suits your needs best. My personal choice has been Kindle Direct Publishing (or KDP). I find their website easy to use, their process relatively pain-free, royalties and author copy cost reasonable and competitive. Because I've not used other platforms, I cannot speak with any authority on their merits, and even if I did, I'd still tell you to research several before deciding.

If you choose KDP, you'll have an option to use a free ISBN, assigned by KDP, in publishing your book, or you can purchase your own. Using their ISBN limits you to distribution only through them. This is perfectly fine, however, know that at the time of this publication, bookstores and libraries are less likely to shelve your books because of the publisher being 'Independently published.' I have been using their assigned ISBN numbers up until now, however, I plan to purchase my own for some future publications to see if there's a significant difference in sales.

Hopefully, you're finding this all to be not so scary or confusing. However, if you are, remember there is always plenty of help out there to walk you through. Let's move on to the next phase.

HIGHLIGHTS

Do your homework. There are several great quality independent publishing platforms to choose from, each with its own pros and cons.

ISBN knowledge. Understanding the function of your ISBN number and your options will save you aggravation.

Not that the story need be long, but it will take a long while to make it short.
— Henry David Thoreau

7 ANCHORS AWEIGH

As you finish up your final details with your book, you'll want to have a book launch—or book release—date set and announced. Congratulations, your book is ready to set sail. Typically, new books launch on Tuesdays. It's a longtime practice that seems to relate to ease of distribution, leveling the playing field for authors in regard to best sellers list, and some other reason that is sort of irrelevant for our purposes. Just…Tuesdays. If you're not shooting for a best sellers list, then by all means, do as you wish.

Whatever you decide for a launch date, you should be promoting it on your website and across your social media accounts (which you've been diligently posting to and building up hype for your new release, right?) Building excitement and anticipation will drive sales.

If you haven't already, this is a great time to start considering where and how you'd like to launch your book release party. Most typically, it would be a bookstore or library. It will be your responsibility to engage their interest in you and your book. Before you do, though, have some marketing materials in hand.

Here are some of the most common self-promotion materials for authors:

- **Business cards**. Whether you have a logo or use your book cover design, be sure to have your website, social media, and email contact info visible.
- **Bookmarks**. Bookmarks are a favorite. The same idea applies as with business cards.
- **Pens**. Not necessary, but a nice touch.
- **Book Related Memento**. If your book is

about a baseball player, perhaps baseball bat keychains (or helmet) or even baseball card styled business cards. Be creative. Again, not necessary, but a nice touch that'll make you stand out.

Go in (with books and swag) and introduce yourself. Ask if they'd be willing to host your book launch. They'll need to know what's in for them, so let them know how you plan on drawing a crowd. Don't be afraid to think outside of the box, either. If your book is set at a vineyard, or a café or your main character is a beer lover, approach those types of venues. For example, one of my book launches was held at a coffee shop that I mentioned in the book.

So, how do you get people to show up? Well, as I mentioned, building your social media presence is the fastest (and cheapest) way. Once you've secured your location and date, create a Facebook event and invite people on your friend's list. I suggest you also 'boost 'the event—which you pay for and can cost as little as five dollars—to your surrounding towns and cities, or target people who are interested in your topic.

Contact your local community newspaper

journalist and ask them to cover your book launch. Use your status as a local or a native to the town as a point of interest. In the same vein, many towns have an online community newspaper that accepts contributor articles and event postings. Use these to share your press release and post your event. Be sure to read up on how to write a press release if you have never done so. While they are quite easy to do, there are some rules of thumb to follow.

You'll want to have those business cards, bookmarks, and some kind of banner (be it cardboard or vinyl) to hand out and display. If you have one book, using your cover image is perfect. Candy or mints are a nice touch, too. Your host may or may not have a table for you to use, so make sure you know ahead of time what you'll need to bring. I always bring my own tablecloth and a runner with my logo, too.

If you plan on writing more books, you'll want to consider 'branding' yourself. For example, I have numerous books out, and I also blog (infrequently these days) on my website. My tagline is "Finding Beauty in the Imperfections of Life,' and my logo is a cartoon depiction of me holding a book. Take some time to think about what represents you/your work/your message and go from there.

Now for a little truth-bomb. Local, unknown

authors do not often draw a big crowd. If the only people who show up for your launch are your friends and family, don't be discouraged. This happens to all of us. Use them as your chance to practice the dreaded 'elevator pitch' and give a reading. (We'll talk about those soon) Then, shake it off and move on to the next opportunity. Please, don't waste a single moment on perceived fails. Keep your eyes trained ahead for successes.

I mentioned 'elevator pitch' and giving a book reading. At any and every book signing event you attend, you'll be asked, "What is your book about?" You're going to need an answer for that, and a good one.

I've heard authors give long, exhausting, detailed descriptions with blow by blow narratives, and I've seen authors freeze and mumble. Be prepared to talk about your book in concise, engaging, brief description. Entice them, tease them, don't bore them or give them the whole story. In a nutshell, you're giving them the back of the book description, so study that, and you'll be fine.

Side note. I have one particular book—Lost and Found Girls—that I give the most pathetic elevator pitch for. It's been out for at least two years, and I still struggle with describing it. Mostly, it's because the shocking turning point comes early in the book, and I don't know what to say to not give away the moment. Until I figure it out, I'm just saying it's a "hauntingly strange tale of two young girls who'll take you on a journey of love, loss, redemption and faith." Then, I apologize for giving such a vague description and I tell them why I did so. I'm honest to a fault, I guess. Ironically, I know in my heart it's a great story, one that came out of nowhere and still one of my favorites and deserves to be read.

SWAG GUIDE

The purpose of swag is marketing. Yes, it's a bummer to give away stuff you've spent your hard-earned money on. But if you're serious about getting yourself out there, it helps.

You don't have to break the bank. Companies like Vistaprint offer everything from business cards to banners and virtually everything in between.

Bookmarks are always a safe bet. Have your book or brand logo clearly visible, as well as your website, social media, and email.

Shop around. This is the time to be a bargain hunter. You want the most bang for your buck, and to always be well stocked.

Swag crazy. Some authors—like me—love their swag. I offer a lot of goodies to buyers. This is absolutely not necessary... but it's fun.

Ideas: wristbands, playing cards, pens, notepads, keychains, mints, chocolates, bookmarks, lapel pins, and more. All should have your logo/book name and website.

I have been successful probably because I have always realized that I knew nothing about writing and have merely tried to tell an interesting story entertainingly.
— Edgar Rice Burroughs

8 NAVIGATING THE CIRCUIT

I relayed that story because it's important to understand that there are few rules here, and mostly guidelines. There is only one thing I would say is imperative, though. *Be authentic.* You should avoid trying to 'sales pitch' anyone, you should be trying to *connect* with them.

So, now that you've launched your book and

had your first taste of what we authors do, you're ready to start attending book signing events. You can find them through social media, libraries, fair and festival listing websites, churches, and your local author groups. They are especially abundant in the fall and pre-holidays. Consider offering yourself to book clubs as well and entice them with a free book for the host, or a gift basket giveaway.

Not unlike your book launch, you'll need to bring your arsenal of 'goodies.' I like to be over prepared. Most events expect you to bring your own table and will provide a chair (unless it's an outdoor event, then bring your own chair, too). Have plenty of books on hand to sell (power of positive thinking), a bare minimum of twenty. Make sure you have pens for signing books and change for sales, as well as a credit card reader. Post a small sign on your table letting buyers know you accept credit cards. Have a beverage on hand and a snack. Have book stands to display your book(s) and keep your table clear of clutter. Make it look clean, engaging, and inviting. Say hello to your vendor neighbors, and if there's time, go around and introduce yourself. Bring business cards to hand out, and ask them for theirs as well.

Now you're ready for your event. There are some do's and don'ts of engaging prospective readers. As with everything I write, this is my personal opinion, based on my experiences.

- **Don't be pushy.** I've seen authors badger and trap prospective readers with a canned speech—it's the one they give every single passerby—to the point where they just buy the book to make them stop talking. Sure, the author may have made the sale, and if they only plan on releasing one book, I guess that's good enough. But *I* want people to buy my book because they're genuinely interested. I want them to become fans. Fans who'll follow my social media accounts and watch for my next release to come out.
- **Don't be a wallflower.** Conversely, I've seen authors sit behind their table and their books and all but refuse to engage with anyone. They sell zero books, make no connections, and pack up and leave at the end of the event without a word. Believe me, I 'get' introversion. I understand feeling nervous,

uncomfortable, and awkward.
- **Do find the middle.** If you want to get your books into readers hands, you have to find somewhere in the middle. Be assertive, not aggressive. Friendly, not overbearing.
- **Do price your books within the market.** Don't overprice. See what books in your genre and page length are going for and be competitive with that.
- **Do be approachable and friendly.** No one wants to chat up a sourpuss, or someone who won't look up from their phone.

With all that said, to each their own, of course. If pitching spiels are in your comfort zone, go for it. I can only tell you how it comes across. If sitting quietly behind your table and hoping someone will buy a book without talking to you, go for it... *I can only tell you how it comes across*. The hard truth is, the only time you're going to get a pass on being aloof or hyper-assertive is if you're already famous. If you've ever heard the saying about how wealthy people who behave oddly are called eccentric, whereas a poor person with the same behavior is simply weird, then you understand.

YOU WROTE IT, NOW WHAT?

I've read that in our world—the author's world—there are upwards of three hundred thousand books published (new titles and re-editions) annually. That's just in the United States. It doesn't make it impossible to grow your readership, it just makes it hard. Don't let that deter you. Your book was important enough for you to write, so it deserves a fighting chance to be seen.

This is why joining the convention circuit, fairs, and festivals, and author events are so important. Connect with your potential audience. Give them someone they can relate to. When you sit behind your table, you are no longer Tom Smith, you are *Author Tom Smith*. Have a presence. Dress the part. Give them a reason to want to stop and talk to you.

Even still, they may walk away without buying a book. Don't be discouraged. Do make sure they've left with your business card (or bookmark, postcard, etc.) or signed up for your mailing list. Some in our field will tell you that if you didn't make the sale in person at the moment, they never will buy. I disagree. I have made many post-event sales from readers who later tell me that they couldn't stop thinking about our conversation, or a particular book cover, or whatever the case was. Sometimes it's as simple as they wanted the ebook instead of the paperback. Don't underestimate the value of connecting with people.

The great news is that there are plenty of great conversation openers to engage prospective readers. Some suggestions:

- **Ask** them: "What kind of books do you like to read?" Chances are, you find something relatable in your book. And if not, it's okay to say so. Follow it up with a simple, "Well, if you know anyone who's a fan of _____, I've just the book for them.
- **Compliment** them on something they're wearing. Be sincere, though. I'd never tell someone, 'I love your scarf' if I thought it hideous.
- **Remind** them that signed books make great gifts.

Spontaneous conversations with strangers aren't just for extroverts. Treat everyone you meet as a dear friend. Look them in the eye, listen to what they say, be present. They will buy, or they won't. At a recent vendor fair, an elderly woman came by. I greeted her, told her I write contemporary fiction, mainly geared toward women. She was, at best, mildly interested. She saw the cover of my book Mae's Café, and said, "Oh, I had an Aunt Mae."

I had a fairly good idea she wasn't really interested in buying anything from me, but since she'd commented on the cover, I told her a little about where it came from. I explained that the name popped into my head as I thought about this character who loved everything nineteen forties. I then added that I created the character because of *my* love of that particular era, especially the movies of the time.

I had the great pleasure of spending nearly a half hour talking old movies and silver screen stars with her, and we both were so gratified to have had the experience of sharing a mutual love. She left without buying a book.

The vendor next to me cringed and said, "Man, it sucks when you spend all that time with them and they don't buy." I laughed and shrugged, agreeing. But then the truth dawned on me, and I told him that I'd loved every second of our conversation. My time wasn't wasted by a chatty, non-buyer. I was given an encounter. Incidentally, and much to my surprise, the woman came back a couple of hours later. She said that she'd gone all the way home but couldn't stop thinking about the book. It was a very sweet surprise.

In summary, be approachable, know what you want to say about your book, and be yourself (just, you know, your best version of yourself). If it's awkward for you to 'people,' then affect your author persona and let him/her take over.

FYI

There is almost always a fee for participating in multi-author/vendor events. The range varies from $10 to upwards of $150 for a single day event. Personally, I usually never spend more than $50 for a single day event, unless I have on good authority it is an especially good selling opportunity.

"I love an author the more for having been himself a lover of books."
  – Henry Wadsworth Longfellow

9 NAVIGATING THE CIRCUIT, PART TWO

Now that we've covered some of the basics for dealing with the public at book signing events, let's talk about our author peers. As a whole, the author community is exceptionally friendly and welcoming. In fact, some of my staunchest supporters are author friends who've I've met 'on the circuit.'

Writing, as you know, is a very isolated and isolating process. You spend hours upon hours working alone, living inside your head, and engaging with the world less than most other professions. I used to be perfectly content—perhaps even pleased—by this. However, once I began to meet and chat with fellow authors, a whole new world opened up. I've learned so much in such a relatively short time, and it's greatly due to the amazing 'author tribe' I've become a part of.

It has also opened incredible opportunities, as well. Shortly before an author's convention—New England Authors Expo—a fellow author reached out to me and asked if I'd be interested in joining his author panel discussion, topic undecided. I went against every natural introvert reaction and said yes. It would be my first ever speaking engagement, and I was terrified.

I'm relieved to say the panel went perfectly. The amazing part was that I *enjoyed* it. Big time. So much so, that I knew immediately that it was a calling. In fact, it was the calling that led to this book, my workshops, and the consulting I now do with aspiring writers.

At the same event, I agreed to participate in a YouTube channel show called, "Tell Me About Your Damn Book," with the awesome Stephen Lomer (who is also an author). Stephen interviews fellow authors and as you can guess, we tell him (and the viewers) about our damn book. It was ridiculously fun and an unbelievable opportunity that dropped in my lap for one reason. I was receptive.

You must be receptive and accepting of opportunity when it appears. Letting shyness or insecurity stop your forward momentum would be a huge disservice to yourself and your work. Say yes, even when it scares you to do so.

Since then, I've gone on to attend many more events and conferences, appeared on podcast interviews and newspaper interviews, created the You Wrote It, Now What workshop, and continued to publish my books. If that sounds like a lot of 'yay me' going on, it is. I'm damn proud of what I've accomplished in short order. However, I still have much to learn and areas to grow in. Pride and humility should always walk hand in hand. Believe me, I've had my ass handed to me as well as praise.

How this all relates to you is this: Take it all in. Take every opportunity. *Create* opportunity. Think outside of the box. Keep your eyes and your mind trained ahead and let no one or nothing stop you. When setbacks and disappointments happen—and they will happen—give yourself a five-minute pity party and move on.

Out of all the advice I could give you, I stress this most of all: Build your own author tribe. This is where you'll turn most often for marketing ideas, book signing events, and emotional support. From them, you'll learn what to do... *and* what not to do.

As an example: At a recent book signing event hosting multiple authors, there was one who failed to use proper author etiquette (I made up the phrase, but it is definitely a thing). This author had a nasty habit of poaching (or trying to) other authors visitors. Poachers are easy to recognize.

- **They call attention away from fellow authors.**
- **They insert themselves into author/visitor conversations.**
- **They call direct attention to themselves at the expense of the other authors.**
- **Their displays encroach on their neighbors**

As well as a host of other obnoxious behaviors. Don't be that author, ever. If it hasn't already, this behavior will eventually bite them—or you if you chose to employ those methods—in the biscuits at some point.

In short, if you choose to view other authors as your competition, your experience will not be a fulfilling one. Conversely, if you choose to treat your fellow authors as colleagues and friends, your experience will be positive.

Also, be generous in your praise and recommendations of fellow authors. If you write contemporary fiction but a visitor to your table tells you they only read mystery, then send them over to an author who writes that genre. Chances are, they'll reciprocate when the time comes.

Sometimes at multi-author events, you'll find that fellow authors may ask if you want to 'swap' books of the same value. This is purely up to you, there is no right response. Although to be perfectly honest, I've yet to find a tactful way out of it when I'm not interested.

If you do accept the swap (or purchase another author's book) be sure to review it for them on their site of preference. Typically, it would be Amazon and Goodreads. Don't be shy about asking them to do the same. When reviewing a book on any platform, keep in mind that a three-star review is considered a negative review and will drop an author's ratings. A five-star review does not mean you thought the book was perfect, just that you really liked it.

My personal rule of thumb is that if I cannot give a four or five-star review, I don't leave one at all. I've yet to have that happen, though. FYI—you'll be spending much of your author's life trying to get people to review your book for you.

"A writer is someone for whom writing is more difficult than it is for other people."
--Thomas Mann, Essays of Three Decades

10 OVERALL PRESENTATION

We've addressed the key factors in a making a book signing event a positive experience. How you engage with prospective readers and with fellow authors is entirely up to you and my recommendations are based on nearly one hundred events at the time of publishing this book.

No matter what the circumstances—a lousy sales day or a great sales day—going in optimistic and open to all possibilities will keep you in a healthy frame of mind. I've had times when one person has shown up and times when I've sold out of my supply. It's always going to be hit or miss, and typically, the times you think will be great are a bust, and the times your expectations are very low are the best.

The one thing that should remain consistent is your presentation and representation of yourself. As you do more and more events, odds are, people will start to recognize you. Especially if you've been working the social media and self-promoting end of your business. Who and what do you want them to see?

In my personal life, you can find me most often in baggy, harem-style pants and comfy tops. I suppose I'm a bit of a flower-child—mellow, easy breezy, nature-loving—minus the drugs. In my professional life, I'm a bit more put-together... looking. My personality is the same, my appearance is different. I sincerely enjoy giving my prospective readers an experience.

My table display, business cards, banner, bookmarks, pens, and more are flowery and pretty. I have lots of swag for them to choose from, as well as chocolates and mints. Often times I'll stand to talk to them. I'm like the Olive Garden of authors... *When you're with me, you're with family*. Yes, I'm being slightly facetious, but you get the point, I'm sure.

The way I do things is natural to *me*. What I do may not feel comfortable or right for you. Whatever you decide to do, make it meaningful to you and your book/brand. As long as it's relevant to what you've written, you'll attract whoever belongs in your readership.

"Get it down. Take chances. It may be bad, but it's the only way you can do anything really good."
— William Faulkner

11 YOU'RE READY

While there are so many moving parts to writing, publishing, and promoting your book, the constant is *you*. As an independently published author, you get all the control *and* all the responsibility. Even if you become traditionally published—particularly with a small publishing house—you will still need to do the majority of marketing and promotion. It is as wonderful as it is exhausting.

I put a tremendous amount of work and effort into building my brand and increasing my exposure. It's true that, sometimes, I wonder why the hell I bother. Then, someone will reach out to me and say my book affected them. Or that I inspired them to continue writing. That's when I remember my why.

You're going to need to have a clear understanding of *your* why as you navigate your writing journey. There will be times when you feel like you're just spinning in your proverbial hamster wheel or treading water. Odds are you'll be in the red for a while and not see a profit. It will be discouraging and disheartening.

AND NOW FOR THE PEP TALK

Don't quit. As I said before, if it was important enough for you to write it, it deserves a chance to be seen. I can tell you, you'll never get tired of saying and knowing that *you are an author*. It was a dream that became a goal, that became a reality.

Whatever it is that may be holding you back, let it go. Be forewarned—I'm about to drop a cliché on you—you should live like you are dying. Is that a bit morbid? Maybe, but I know you understand. Time is one of the most precious things we have. Don't waste it on fear or insecurity. It's not your job to worry about what anyone else thinks of you or your work.

Your job is to put out work *you* believe in, even if it seems like no one else does. If you've published a book, you've already done more than someone who's just talked about it. You've got some street cred to add to your swagger. Just keep plugging along, and what will be will be.

Contrary to all the above is another side of the coin. It's okay to be fine with just publishing a book. It really is. Don't want to market and promote? Don't. Have zero interest in book shows and events? Don't go to them. If you want to just mention it to friends, family, and acquaintances at dinner parties, go for it.

Literary renown, fame, financial growth as a result of book sales may not be your goal. Maybe simply publishing it was. Only you can decide your journey, and whatever you do, you've made the right choice. If you decide somewhere down the road that you're interested in promoting your book, you could always re-release it and go from there.

People will come at you from all directions with advice and suggestions and maybe they'll be right or maybe they'll be wrong. None of them are you, though.

I'm so excited for you as you embark on your writing career and I hope I've helped you in some way. I love communicating with my readers, so feel free to reach out to me at authorelsakurt@gmail.com with any feedback you may have. Remember, authors need reviews to be seen, so if you liked the book, visit my Amazon Author page (or Goodreads) and leave a review! Best wishes on your journey and I look forward to seeing you in print!

It's none of their business that you have to learn to write. Let them think you were born that way.
— Ernest Hemingway

12 FINAL NOTES

The last thing I'd like to leave you with is a compilation of resources I have used and use as of publishing this book. I receive no compensation for sharing these resources, nor can I guarantee your satisfaction with their services or products.

For writing, I use Microsoft Word—mostly because it's what I currently know best. Scrivener, Pages, and many more programs and software are available, and pricing varies.

For editing, and writing improvement I use Grammarly, Hemingway, and Master Writer.

For publishing, I use Kindle Direct Publishing, formerly Createspace. Ingram Spark, Xlibris, Kobo, and many more are popular as well. I do intent to try Ingram Spark in the near future.

For social media, I most often use Facebook, Instagram, Twitter, and Pinterest (in that order or frequency). I also use Goodreads, Amazon Author Central, and Goodreads with regularity. For my website, I use WordPress.

For my graphic design needs, I use Canva, Ripl, and Luna Pic. For video creating and editing, I use AVS video, which is free at the time of this publication.

My promotional materials needs are met by Vistaprint, Zazzle, Amazon, Best of Signs, Oriental Trading Company, and Teespring. Promotion assistance comes from KDP rocket and AMS. Additional training and further education come most often from Kindlepreneur and Udemy.

I find most of my events through social media, my state author's association, fellow authors, local bookstores and libraries, and fair and festival finder websites.

Consider these resources as starting points for each phase of your writing journey, but not as your writer's bible. New resources are always cropping up and merit looking into. Most beginning authors are on a tight budget, so spend wisely, Again, I cannot recommend or guarantee your satisfaction with any of the listed services or products other than to say I have personally been satisfied.

If I could leave you with one last thing, it is this. No matter what you do, whose advice you take, or how and when you achieve your goals, keep these 'success' stories in mind. As you'll see, true success is a road paved with failure.

From Unknown Source:

"At age 23, **Tina Fey** was working at a YMCA.

At age 23, **Oprah** was fired from her first reporting job.

At age 24, **Stephen King** was working as a janitor and living in a trailer.

At age 27, **Vincent Van Gogh** failed as a missionary and decided to go to art school.

At age 28, **J.K. Rowling** was a suicidal single

parent living on welfare.

At age 28, **Wayne Coyne** (from The Flaming Lips) was a fry cook.

At age 30, **Harrison Ford** was a carpenter.

At age 30, **Martha Stewart** was a stockbroker.

At age 37, **Ang Lee** was a stay-at-home-dad working odd jobs.

Julia Child released her first cookbook at age 39 and got her own cooking show at age 51.

Vera Wang failed to make the Olympic figure skating team, didn't get the Editor-in-Chief position at Vogue and designed her first dress at age 40.

Stan Lee didn't release his first big comic book until he was 40.

Alan Rickman gave up his graphic design career to pursue acting at age 42.

Samuel L. Jackson didn't get his first movie role until he was 46.

Morgan Freeman landed his first MAJOR movie role at age 52.

Kathryn Bigelow only reached international success when she made The Hurt Locker at age 57.

Grandma Moses didn't begin her painting career until age 76.

Louise Bourgeois didn't become a famous artist until she was 78.

"Whatever your dream is, it is not too late to achieve it. You aren't a failure because you haven't found fame and fortune by the age of 21. Hell, it's okay if you don't even know what your dream is yet. Even if you're flipping burgers, waiting tables or answering phones today, you never know where you'll end up tomorrow. Never tell yourself you're too old to make it. Never tell yourself you missed your chance. Never tell yourself that you aren't good enough. ***You can do it. Whatever it is."***

YOU WROTE IT, NOW WHAT?

If you have been given this book as part of Elsa Kurt's presentation of **'You Wrote It, Now What?'** please use the following pages for notes.

YOU WROTE IT, NOW WHAT?

ELSA KURT

ABOUT THE AUTHOR

Elsa Kurt is a multi-genre, indie & traditionally published author, brand designer, and speaker. She currently has eight novels independently published, as well as three novellas published with Crave Publishing in their Craving: Country, Craving: Loyalty, and Crave: Billionaire's Club anthologies. She is a lifelong New England resident and married mother of two grown daughters. When not writing, designing, or talking her head off, she can be found gardening, hiking, kayaking, and just about anywhere outdoors. Or, you could just find Elsa on social media:
https://facebook.com/authorelsakurt/
https://instagram.com/authorelsakurt/
https://twitter.com/authorelsakurt
https://bit.ly/2RbvOBz
https://allauthor.com/profile/elsakurt/
https://amazon.com/author/elsakurt
https://www.pinterest.com/authorelsakurt/pins/
and her website, https://www.elsakurt.com

Made in United States
North Haven, CT
30 June 2023

38411298R00046